Remarriage and Adultery In the Bible

Michael S. Sayen

Published in Forest Lake, MN

Christy Bieber, J.D. in *Forbes Advisor,* stated that, "63% of divorcees believe a better understanding of the commitments of marriage could have helped them to avoid divorce."

For the time will come when they will not endure sound doctrine, but according to their own desires, because they have itching ears, they will heap up for themselves teachers; and they will turn their ears away from the truth, and be turned aside to fables. – 2 Timothy 4:3-4

First Edition

Email: mikesayen@hotmail.com

Printed in the U.S.A.

Testimonials

"This well-researched work, especially from Jewish sources, sheds light on the divorce/remarriage issue that today has been neglected by the church due to cultural assimilation. Re-examining the crucial biblical texts is a necessary spiritual concern for believers in an age where such examination is dismissed on grounds that since pastors disagree, no one can attempt to apply these texts today. This work answers this need in a direct and easy to understand approach." – **Dr. Randall Price, Distinguished Research Professor, Liberty University**

"Michael Sayen's study on marriage and remarriage is one of the most thoughtful and challenging pieces of research that I have seen on this topic." – **Gary R. Habermas, Philosophy Department, Liberty University. One of the world's leading experts on the Resurrection of Christ.**

"Michael Sayen has dug deeply into Scripture to uncover the biblical teaching on divorce and remarriage. It takes a courageous and openminded scholar to take on such a task. I have appreciated Michael's careful research, clarity of presentation and willingness to modify his personal view based on new information. I recommend this book for those who want to take a serious look at this most important, but often perplexing subject." – **Dr. J. Carl Laney, author of "The Divorce Myth: A Biblical Examination of Divorce and Remarriage"**

"Well written and documented. A great resource for pastors and counselors." – **Dr. Daniel A. Berry, Nazarene Bible College, Adjunct Instructor, Pastoral Ministries**

"Sometimes it seems that the Church is as confused as the Pharisees regarding the matter of divorce. Here is a great study on what the Bible actually says including what Jesus taught." – **Dr. James R. Russom, DMin., Nazarene Bible College, Director Pastoral Ministries Programs**

"Fundamentally, I very much appreciate your thoughts and agree with your conclusions. The Christian church, over the centuries, has rendered marriage a caricature of its original intent and potential, with its rampant divorce and remarriage. The secular world looks at this pattern and rightfully wonders what difference a Judeo-Christian value system really makes, let alone what benefit it provides." – **Ingo Sorke, Ph.D., Hospice Chaplain**

"This is an interesting read. Arguing that Jesus' and other NT writers' teaching on divorce (and the possibility of a remarriage) is based on the Jewish understanding, which places all authority and responsibility for decisions on divorce upon the husband, Sayen's work goes against the grain of most contemporary Christian thought on the issue. After reading this thought provoking and paradigm-shifting work, believers will have a lot to ponder on the issue, the most pertinent question being this: have we misread the Bible on the question of divorce and remarriage?" – **Jeremiah Mutie, Th.M., Ph.D., Southern California Seminary, Professor of Theology and Church History**

"This book captures the Old Testament theological and civil view on marriage in a way the reader can understand." – **Pastor Brett Peterson, Ph.D., Living Water Community Church, Biblical Studies**

"Thank you for your studied teaching on this subject. We need sound clear teaching on this subject and you are providing it." – **Dr. Keith J. Wise, History/Religion, Alma College**

"You did a thorough work on the subject, particularly regarding the Jewish background regarding marriage and divorce. In my opinion, that is the strength of your arguments as Jesus and Paul sided with the Jewish view in opposition to the current cultural views of the day." – **Dr. Bob McKay (Missionary) Georgia, Former Soviet Union**

"We cannot allow culture to be the lens through which truth is imparted, otherwise truth is merely the vote of the masses." – **Dr. Joseph Davis (Southeastern University) Professors of Religion**

iii

*"I could find no theological errors in your work, and your reasoning from scripture seems ironclad, however, there must be room for grace and forgiveness for past sins." – **Dr. William Watson, Colorado Christian University, Professor of Global History**

*"This book is well written; the academic prose should not put anyone off, as this is a serious subject matter. I found the discussion helpful and the conclusions put forward respectfully and with further discussion in mind. Recommended!" – **Rev. Robert Saler Ph.D, Christian Theological Seminary, Executive Director of the Center for Pastoral Excellence**

*"I thought it was especially relevant to emphasize how counter-cultural the Biblical view of marriage would have been to the Gentiles as the Judeo-Christian ethic challenged their assumptions and practices. It seems to me that this background is vital to interpreting Paul's teachings on marriage and divorce. I agree with your analysis of Matthew and Mark's accounts of Jesus' teaching on divorce and adultery particularly as it addresses the exception clause question. I also agree that you have correctly analyzed Paul's teaching in the relevant Corinthian passages." – **M.Div. Ronnie J. Woolard, Mid-Atlantic Christian University, Professor of Bible**

*"Such a hard topic in today's culture and climate. Your theology is accurate. I feel the church has an incredible opportunity to minister and provide. It is a time for the church to be the light in the darkness!" – **Jon Moton, Central Christian Church, Campus Pastor, Ahwatukee Campus**

*"You have written an excellent explanation of Biblical marriage. Every pastor should read this and give it to every couple before marriage." – **Bill Gothard, BillGothard.com**

*"I don't agree with some of your ideas, but they are within the realm of possibility." – **Dr. Ben Witherington III (Asbury Theological Seminary) Jean R. Amos Professor of New Testament for Doctrinal Studies**

Foreword

In a day when culture has abandoned God's teachings on women, marriage, and many other cultural issues, it is refreshing to read such work. Current cultural views have become so ingrained that few would listen to a biblical explanation. The issues facing marriage and divorce are not new. Abuse, immorality, and multiple marriages have always been with us. They are now so rampart that they have risen to the level of "new normal." Returning to a time when marriage was taken seriously and divorce was stigmatized would be difficult, if not impossible. However, the degradation of society is not an excuse to give up. We must teach biblical views in our homes, churches, and Christian schools. The result may create an "Amaish-style" subculture, but that has always been the case of godliness in society. The application of this will be daunting.

Dean David Lackey, D.Min., Ed.D.
(Clarks Summit University) School of Theology

The Nature of Men and Women

Genesis 3:14 So the Lord God said to the serpent:
"Because you have done this, you are cursed more than all cattle, and more than every beast of the field; on your belly you shall go, and you shall eat dust all the days of your life. 15 And I will put enmity between you and the woman, and between your seed and her Seed; He shall bruise your head, and you shall bruise His heel."

God **humbled** the serpent making him craw in the cursed dust.
Good (perspective): His seed will bruise the heel of her Seed.
Bad (perspective): Her Seed shall bruise the head of his seed.

Genesis 3:16 To the woman He said:
"I will greatly multiply your sorrow and your conception; in pain you shall bring forth children; your desire shall be for your husband, and he shall rule over you."

God **humbled** the woman by giving her pain in child bearing.
Good: Woman will desire a husband to produce children with.
Bad: The man she desires to marry will exercise rule over her.

Genesis 3:17 Then to Adam He said:
"Because you have heeded the voice of your wife, and have eaten from the tree of which I commanded you, saying, 'You shall not eat of it': "Cursed is the ground for your sake; In toil you shall eat of it all the days of your life. 18 Both thorns and thistles it shall bring forth for you, and you shall eat the herb of the field. 19 In the sweat of your face you shall eat bread till you return to the ground, for out of it you were taken; for dust you are, And to dust you shall return."

God **humbled** the man by giving him pain in harvesting food.
Good: Man was taken from the dust of the earth that gave life.
Bad: Man will return to the dust cursed with disease and death.

Introduction

Often, wedding customs and traditions assist in setting the foundation of a marriage.[1] Jews believe that men will exercise dominance over women (Genesis 3:16). The term patriarchy (*the rule of the father*) was used as feminist propaganda against long-standing coverture law that grew in popularity around the time no-fault divorce statues (1969) were enacted. John Piper (2012) helped coin the phrase complementarian to combat the negative view of male leadership in the home, church, and society in his sermon, "God created man male and female. What does it mean to be complementarian?" John said:

> The intention with the word 'complementarian' is to locate our way of life between two kinds error: on the one side would be the abuses of women under male domination, and on the other side would be the negation of gender differences where they have beautiful significance...So complementarians resist the impulses of a chauvinistic, dominating, and abusive culture, on the one side, and the impulses of a sex-blind, gender-leveling, unisex culture, on the other side.[2] (para. 3, 4)

---

[1] The Conversation, "How 'Bride Price' Reinforces Negative Stereotypes: a Ghanaian Case Study," accessed March 18, 2021, https://theconversation.com/how-bride-price-reinforces-negative-stereotypes-a-ghanaian-case-study-120337.

[2] John Piper, "God Created Man Male and Female. What Does It Mean to Be Complementarian?", Paragraph 2-3, accessed April 2, 2018, https://www.desiringgod.org/messages/god-created-man-male-and-female-what-does-it-mean-to-be-complementarian.

Coverture ("to cover"), codified at common law in 1765, referred to the legal status of a married woman. It created a legal fiction where the husband and wife were one-flesh and one-blood (unity of person). And that one was the husband. To represent this transfer, his wife took her husband's last name. A married women (*feme covert*) had no rights. The wife could not sign contracts, own land, or cash checks without permission. Children were under the property rights of their father. The Woman's Suffrage Movement began with the intention of dismantling coverture in the mid-nineteenth century (1848). Coverture ended when the Supreme Court declared in U.S. v. Yazell (1966) that, "the institution of coverture is... obsolete."

For most of history, women could not initiate a divorce. The Church of England had jurisdiction over all matrimonial matters and considered marriage an indissoluble sacrament. Divorce required a private act of Parliament. The number of divorces in all of English History was a mere 324. And only four for women.[3] The Matrimonial Causes Act (1857) took all matrimonial jurisdiction away from the ecclesiastical courts so that women could divorce. Women could divorce for adultery, but it must be repetitive and compounded by a second offence.

God betrothed Jerusalem in the wilderness (Jeremiah 2:2). But Israel was divided into two kingdoms (1 Kings 11:32-35). Northern Israel and Southern Judah. God eventually divorced Northern Israel but remained married to Southern Judah (2 Kings 17:20; Jeremiah 3:8-9). Southern Judah was cut-off for rejecting Jesus (Jeremiah 31:32; Acts 3:23; Hebrews 8:9). Christ betrothed the Church to Himself (2 Corinthians 11:2; Revelation 16:9). Did Jesus come to give women equal rights in divorce or to discourage men from divorcing their wife? This book compares the unilateral marriage practices of the Jews to the bilateral culture of the Gentiles in the first century.

---

[3] Smithsonian Magazine, "The Heartbreaking History of Divorce", accessed July 10, 2021, http://www.smithsonianmag.com/history/heart-breaking-history-of-divorce-180949439/.

Marriage and Divorce

A Culture's Concept of Divorce
Three biblical reasons the marriage covenant is unilateral.

- *Acquire = Man acquires his wife with the Bride Price*
- *Adultery = Man has reproductive rights over his wife*
- *Divorce = Only man can divorce (Deuteronomy 24:1)*

Marriage was designed to be a unilateral covenant for life. Jesus addressed adultery with Jews in a monogamous society. Monogamy changed the unilateral acquisition of the woman through the bride price to the bilateral covenant with a dowry. Marriages became conditional covenants without bride prices. Women wanted permission to divorce and bodily autonomy. The point of this book is to help people understand divorce. "You can't really know where you are going until you know where you have been" is a famous quote that couldn't be truer. All major ancient civilizations were at one time polygamous. Ancient Greece was the first major civilization that practiced socially enforced monogamy. Ancient Rome closely followed. Jesus said a man who lusts after a woman commits adultery. He also said, a man who divorces his innocent wife causes her to commit adultery, and he who marries the divorced woman. This meant to shock those who thought they obeyed the law. They thought the certificate gave her permission to remarry. Jesus challenged the cultural understanding of adultery saying that an unfaithful husband commits adultery against his wife. It was unusual for husbands to be called adulterers for having sex with unmarried women (called stuprum in Ancient Rome). At times, this appears to be a covenant of equality with shared responsibilities, "likewise, the husband does not have authority over his own body, but the wife does" (1 Corinthians 7:4). Jesus teaches divorce and remarriage based in their own legal system while still keeping the general rule of man's authority.

Jesus was not calling polygamy unlawful in the Law of Moses. Jesus was simply trying to point out that men are not innocent. Society will never have God's laws perfectly codified. Christians can perform biblical marriage with unbiblical laws. Old Testament marriage is God's design from the beginning. God's desire is seen in Genesis 2:24 and Deuteronomy 24:1. The man "acquires" his wife, and the two become one flesh. God's relationship with Northern Israel and Southern Judah. God was the symbolic husband of the sisters at the same time. God first betrothed Jerusalem in the desert (Jeremiah 2:2). God found Jerusalem as a baby and raised her until it was time for marriage (Ezekiel 16:6). He swore an oath and she became his. Jews were practicing monogamy from the time of Babylon. Jesus simply showed them how to live in an ungodly world. Jews didn't just guess monogamy and get it right before Jesus. And Jesus didn't have them change their laws and customs. This should be a hint. He said, man commits adultery against his wife by being unfaithful to her in divorce and remarriage. It was not something said to the Pharisees in public, but private (Matthew 19:9 was the same account of Mark 10:10-12). Jesus didn't repeat himself. What he said he said to them once, and Mark gives us a little more clarity those he was addressing (Matthew 19:10 Jesus is speaking to his disciples in private. 19:10 was a continuation of 19:9. Jesus starts off, "And I say," like Jesus said to His followers at the Sermon on the Mount).

Jesus said things in private that would be foreign to Jews. Jesus said the woman commits adultery if she divorces her husband and remarries (Mark 10:12). This was not something the Jews were practicing. Mark was written to Jews in Rome. Josephus informs us Jewish women were taking advantage of their legal system in Rome by putting away their husbands. This would not have been repeated in the Gospel of Matthew. Therefore, we can conclude, the private message about divorce and remarriage was to the readers (Jews and Gentiles) according to their culture, and not according to Moses' Law. Jesus was not promoting monogamy; he was promoting faithfulness.

It seems that Christians should not practice polygamy in a monogamous society to bring reproach on the name of Christ (promoting sex outside of marriage). Which seems wrong. We know polygamy is not a sin because the Bible does no call it a sin in the Law of Moses. To Jesus, it was more about being bright lights in our community and promoting faithfulness to wives and husbands. You may disagree, but the church came to the conclusion that polygamy is adultery in the 4th century because of the Gospel accounts of divorce and remarriage. It took a while, but they realized they can't say Jesus promoted a monogamy only message without changing the Mosaic Law.

God was married in polygamy (Jacob, Rachel, and Leah). There were laws surrounding polygamy in the Old Testament. Jacob married the unloved to marry the loved. And Israel was split due to sin and deceit. They were both tricked by sin and had to take a hard hit in marriage. But they did it for the love they had for the chosen bride. True Israel (Jacob for Rachel). The apple of his eye. I am sure if Jesus came today, he would not try and changed family law, but how we practice faithfulness in our families. And if Jesus went to Africa today, Jesus would not tell them to divorce their second or third wife and put away the children born to them. Jesus would not preach monogamy only in a polygamous society. And He would not preach polygamy only in a monogamous society. Jesus would say the same thing he said to us in the Gospels. Don't divorce. But if you put away your wife without the knowledge of sexual immorality, you commit adultery against her if you remarry. And the man who marries your former wife commits adultery. And your former divorced wife commits adultery in marriage. And if a woman divorced her husband and remarried, she would be guilty of adultery. It's all the same message we get. Paul said in 1 Corinthians 7:11 that the woman, not the man, is to remain unmarried or reconcile if she separated from her husband. The man was told not to divorce his wife in vs. 11. He was not commanded to remain unmarried or reconcile. Later, he was told he can marry when loosed from a wife and it would not be a sin (1 Corinthians 7:27-28). The woman was not given the same general message. She was given freedom to remarry after the death of her husband (1 Corinthians 7:29). Chapter seven we get gender specific commands (not neutral). Man has his set laws, being the leader, and woman has her set laws, being under the law (rule) of her husband (Genesis 3:16). The law of the husband prevented a wife from being able to put away her husband and marry another, or being able to take a second husband (polyandry). She was not able to free herself. The Greek word for husband is under-man, showing the reader why woman was under the *law of her husband* (Romans 7:2).

I say to you, whoever divorces his wife, except for sexual immorality, and remarries, commits adultery (Matthew 19:9). Jesus charged believers not to divorce (1 Corinthians 7:10-11). Believers made a lifelong promise to their spouse and to God and should honor that commitment. Jesus commanded men not to separate what God joined together (Matthew 19:6). However, it is important to acknowledge scripture does permit a man to divorce his wife for uncleanness (*sexual immorality*). Unbelievers initiating the separation can also be a valid reason for divorce (1 Corinthians 7:15). Israel and Judah committed adultery (idol worship) against God (Husband). God divorced Israel but stayed married to Judah because she repented though her repentance was in pretense of heart (Jeremiah 3:8-9). God commended backsliding Israel for being more forthright than treacherous Judah. God desires one be hot or cold, but spews lukewarm out of His mouth. Israel was subject to being stoned (complete inhalation) for adultery but the certificate of divorce (cut-off) allowed Israel (a remnant) to survive final judgement. This gives Israel a chance to repent and return in the last days.

Man was given *rule* over his wife (Genesis 3:16) just as the sun rules over the day and the moon rules over the night (Genesis 1:18). Man does not have rule over his wife if she is allowed to divorce her husband and send him out of his home. Jews believe a man acquires his wife through the bride price, and because of this, she is not allowed to divorce her husband.

The tradition of the engagement ring that we practice today came from a mixture of the bride price and pagan practices. Bride prices were traditionally given to the woman's father. However, this changed when Jewish religious leaders adopted the marriage contract (ketubah) to lower the bride price on the front end that promised unlawfully divorced woman financial protections on the back end. The ring was already in practice by pagans since ancient times in Egypt (and Greece & Rome). In Rome, a gold ring symbolized the legal contract that transferred ownership from the father to the husband. Jews lowered the bride price to one silver or copper coin or an item of value. Therefore, it was easy to adopt a gold wedding band to be the item of value required in the Law of Moses in the 10th century. The marriage contract (ketubah) started to record a dowry the woman brought to the marriage shortly after the time of Jesus. The Catholic Church authorized the betrothal ring in 1215. Archduke Maximilian recorded the first diamond ring in 1477. In the United States, many states required the engagement ring to be returned back to the giver as a condition of marriage. Bride price evolved over time as monogamy became the gold standard in the church (condemning polygamy). The dowry (money given by the bride's family to the husband) naturally replaced the bride price in enforced monogamous societies. Bilateral contracts in forced monogamous societies promoted equality which eventually gave women permission to divorce. After monogamy was enforced in any culture, women began to divorce men and started to enter the workforce, liberating men from working by the sweat of the brow as sole providers.

Tirzah Meacham (leBeit Yoreh) in "The Legal-Religious Status of the Married Woman" (2009) said divorce cannot be effected by civil courts or religious institutions, "Due to the nature of kiddushin [betrothal] as a unilateral acquisition of the woman, a married woman is always at a legal disadvantage in reference to her personal freedom.... Because the man unilaterally acquires the woman, only he can release her through divorce" (para 11). In the United States we practice bilateral marriage and unilateral divorce. In a bilateral marriage, both parties exchange promises (vows). And with no-fault divorce one person *unilaterally* divorces their spouse without fault. This violates contract law. Bilateral contracts terminated unilaterally without fault lack proper consideration (this for that). In the Old Testament, only the man was allowed to initiate a divorce because he acquired his wife through the bride price. The woman could not initiate divorce because her husband had rule over her (Genesis 3:16). In the Old Testament, we observe fathers having complete authority over their daughters. But Jewish customs allow daughters to partake in the consideration by giving them a chance to ratify the covenant in acceptance. Legally, a contract is not breached unless a promise is broken. The covenant (promise) she entered into (accepted) required her to be sexually faithful (performance) to her husband as long as he lived. The man promises the woman's father that he will take his daughter as a wife (and perform the duties of a husband). Moses, therefore, allowed man to put away his wife for uncleanness because her body belonged *exclusively* to him, and fornication (sexual immorality) was a breach against that one flesh performance (consummation). The woman did not make a promise to be married to one man (Romans 7:1-5) obey her husband (Genesis 3:16) or be bound (1 Corinthians 7:39). Unilateral marriage is a promise for performance agreement. He *promises* marriage, and she accepts through *performance.*

Knowing what Jesus taught about divorce and remarriage was not an easy task for the early believers (Matthew 19:10). For the first four hundred years, the early church seldom allowed divorce and almost unanimously forbade remarriage.[4]

---

[4] Some of the early church fathers allowed a man to initiate the divorce for adultery, but forbid the remarriage of divorced women while their husband still lived. See Bercot, *A Dictionary of Early Christian Beliefs* (Peabody, Massachusetts: Hendrickson Publishers, Inc., 1998). Ambrosiaster, a relatively unimportant church father of the fourth century said, "A woman is not allowed to marry, if she has sent away her husband because of his fornication or apostasy or if, impelled by lust, he is

Jews only permitted man to divorce. According to orthodox Jewish rabbis it was the official position for the State of Israel.[5]

Covenants, Contracts, and Customs

You count the number of promises to determine the type.[6]

- *Bi-lateral (two sides) = Conditional*
- *Uni-lateral (one side) = Unconditional*

Most contracts that people make are bilateral. We form a bilateral contract when we purchase an item at the store, order food at a restaurant, or check a book out at the library. Both parties are mutually obligated by promise in a bilateral contract. But one person is obligated by promise in a unilateral contract. Common unilateral contracts are contests, rewards, and insurance contracts. Unilateral contracts are unconditional (minor *conditions, limitations, and exclusions* may apply).[7] After the offeree performs, the offeror is obligated by promise.

seeking enjoyment of his wife in an illicit way, because the inferior party certainly does not have the same right to this law as the stronger party." He says, however, the man was allowed to remarry if he divorced his wife on the grounds of fornication, "because the husband is not restricted by the law as the woman is, For the head of a woman is her husband." See David Instone-Brewer, *Divorce and Remarriage in the Bible, the Social and Literary Context* (Pre-pub version).

[5] Julie Fineman, "The Importance of a "Get": A Jewish Divorce." accessed April 15, 2021, https://theodysseyonline.com/jewish-divorce.

[6] Encyclopedia.com, "Unilateral Contract," Reference West's Encyclopedia of American Law. Copyright 2005, The Gale Group, Inc. accessed April 15, 2021, http://www.encyclopedia.com/law/encyclopedias-almanacs-transcripts-and-maps/unilateral-contract.

[7] Thismatter.com, "Insurance Contracts: Consideration, Unilateral Contracts (conditional contracts)," William C. Spaulding, accessed September 25, 2017, http://thismatter.com/money/insurance/insurance-contracts.htm.

Divorce is initiated by the husband.[8] Susan Weiss (2009) in a Jewish Encyclopedia quotes Professor Zev Falk saying divorce is, "an 'arbitrary,' unilateral private act of the husband." The Sanhedrin (Jewish ruling body) integrated a written form of the marriage covenant, privately practiced 400 years prior, in the first century BC.[9] Jewish leaders adopted the contract to help men afford getting married and at the same time discourage divorce. It lowered the bride price while offering financial security to widows and unlawfully divorced women. Lamm said in, "The Jewish Marriage Contract (Ketubah)," "The *ketubah* is a unilateral agreement drawn by witnesses in accordance to Jewish civil law, in which they testify that the husband guarantees to his wife that he will meet certain minimum human and financial conditions of the marriage." (n.d., para 1). The marriage contract was signed by the husband and two kosher witnesses. The new bride did not sign the contract.

In the first century, women were granted more financial freedom to manage their own business and financial affairs. Originally, Roman women were under their husband's control which conferred her and all her belongings to her husband and his family. Laws changed allowing women to remain under the legal authority of their father (sine manu) rather than their husband (*in manu*). By staying under their father's authority, the woman was not owned by her husband that afforded her the ability to divorce her husband.[10] Anabaptist Education Today (n.d.) quoted Tertullian, an Early Church Father, saying,

---

[8] Cheris Kramarae & Dale Spender, *Routledge International Encyclopedia of Women: Global Woman's Issues and Knowledge, 1st Edition, The Dependent Woman: Chattel or Person?* (Published in Great Britain by Routledge: Routledge Taylor & Francis Group, New York and London, 2000), 1172.

[9] Jewish Wedding Blog, "The Origins of the Ketubah," accessed April 29, 2024, https://www.jewishwedding101.com/the-origins-of-the-ketubah/.

[10] Stanford University News Service, "Ancient Romans Led the Way in No-fault Divorce," accessed March 17, 2015, http://news.stanford.edu/pr/91/911203Arc1041.html.

"Where is that happiness of married life, ever so desirable, that distinguished our earlier [Roman] manners? As a result of that, for about 600 years there was not among us [Romans] a single divorce. Now [Roman] women have every member of the body heavy laden with gold...and as for divorce, they long for it as though it were the natural consequence of marriage".[11]

Jesus made a unilateral covenant with the Church (called the Bride of Christ).[12] Like Abraham, the promise is one-sided, "Drink from it, all of you. For this is My blood of the new covenant, which is shed for many for the remission of sins." To demonstrate its importance, this was the last time Jesus drank wine with His disciples (Matthew 26:28-29). Jesus took His final sip on the cross, saying, "It is finished!" (John 19:30).

The payment required for the sins of the world was the blood of a perfect sacrifice. Jesus redeemed us with His blood. One flesh in marriage revealed the mystery of Christ and the Church (Ephesians 5:30). "For I have betrothed you to one husband, that I may present you as a chaste virgin to Christ" (2 Corinthians 11:2). Bride price was an important part of marriage. It represented the transfer of authority (Numbers 30:16).

To Cut a Covenant

> "When I passed by you again and looked upon you, indeed your time was the time of love; so I spread My wing over you and covered your nakedness. Yes, I swore an oath to you and entered into a covenant with you, and you became Mine," says the Lord God. – Ezekiel 16:8-9

---

[11] Anabaptist Education Today, "Divorce and Remarriage. What the Early Christians Believed about Divorce and Remarriage NOTES," accessed July 10, 2021, http://anabaptisteducationtoday.wordpress.com/divorce-and-remarriage/.

[12] Cup of wine – Although customs vary, it is important to note both parties traditionally shared the same cup of wine. Matt. 1:19 demonstrates to us that the covenant was made at the betrothal stage, therefore, requiring Joseph to write a writ of divorce to put his betrothed wife away.

The Jews believe a man acquires (similar to purchasing) his wife through the bride price.[13] The man paid a bride price to the young woman's father because he had authority over his daughter in her youth, under his roof. Her father contractually gave his daughter away in marriage. The young woman could not marry without her father's permission because her father had authority over her oaths and promises (Numbers 30:16). He confirms all her vows or makes them void the day that he hears them. Bride price was similar to the purchase price in Scripture (Hosea 3:2). According to the Talmud, the man *acquired* his wife as Abraham *acquired* land (Genesis 23:13). After agreeing to the bride price, the potential groom would drink from the cup of wine and offer it to the young woman. If she drank, that meant she accepted his offer for marriage. They entered into a covenant through the cup of acceptance. Wine represented the blood (called the blood of the grape). Marriage became a covenant by the wine or consummation.[14] His daughter's acceptance satisfied her father's obligations. Betrothed (bound/tied) meant the couple was legally married, which required a writ of divorce to separate (Matthew 1:19). The two became one flesh (Genesis 2:24). Tearing the hymen represented the natural blood covenant (Deuteronomy 22:17).

---

[13] "Understanding that the essence of the marriage lies in a conveyance of a 'property' interest by the bride to the groom serves to explain why it is that only the husband can dissolve the marriage. As the beneficiary of the servitude, divestiture requires the husband's voluntary surrender of the right that he has acquired." see Susan Weiss, "Divorce: The Halakhic Perspective. Jewish Woman: A Comprehensive Historical Encyclopedia," Jewish Woman's Archive, Articles: "Biblical Origins and the Unilateral, No-Fault Grounds for Divorce, Dispensation to Take a Second Wife," accessed October 30, 2017, https://jwa.org/encyclopedia/article/divorce-halakhic-perspective.

[14] Bilateral contracts "morphs" into unilateral contract after the offeree performed. see Dunnell, *Minnesota digest: a digest of the decisions of the Supreme Court of the State of Minnesota covering Minnesota Reports, 1-109, Northwestern Reporter, 1-125* (Owatonna, MN: Minnesota Law Book Co. 1910), 376.

- *Bride Price = Acquired*
- *Betrothal = Covenant*
- *Consummation = One Flesh*

"But if her father overrules her on the day that he hears, then none of her vows or her agreements by which she has bound herself shall stand; and the Lord will release her, because her father overruled her" (Numbers 30:5). A young girl was under her father's authority until marriage, but had full autonomy when divorced or widowed (Number 30:9). Some returned home to their father after a divorce (Leviticus 22:13). Isaac and Rebecca's marriage was arranged by their parents after she agreed to the marriage (Genesis 24:34-51). Isaac took Rebecca into his mother's tent when he saw her, and she became his wife. There was no wedding ceremonies performed or vows exchanged. She became his wife[15] in consummation.[16]

Contracts were a quid pro quo (this for that) agreement. Marriage required proof of an exchange of value for it to exist. Contracts are enforced through courts of law. Covenants are enforced through blood (war or vengeance). Blood for blood. Covenants ratified in blood are enforced through blood. God ratified a promise with a blood oath, "Thus God, determining to show more abundantly to the heirs of promise the immutability of His counsel, confirmed it by an oath" (Hebrews 6:17).

The Hebrew word for covenant is berith. Berith meant agreement, compact, or treaty. Berith was often accompanied by karath. Karath meant to cut, cut out, or cut off. Together, it meant to make an agreement. Abraham *cut* the animals in two, but birds, for God to pass between (Genesis 15:10). The blood

---

[15] Genesis 24:67.

[16] "Then he shall confirm a covenant with many for one week; but in the middle of the week He shall bring an end to sacrifice and offering. And on the wing of abominations shall be one who makes desolate, even until the consummation, which is determined, is poured out on the desolate." Daniel 9:27.

ratified the promise. Abraham *cut* off his flesh in circumcision. In contrast, the bill of divorce was called a *scroll of cutting off.*

- *Karath = To Cut*
- *Sefer k'ritut = Scroll of Cutting Off*

The life of the flesh is in the blood (Leviticus 17:11). Blood symbolized death of the testator. "For where there is a testament, there must also of necessity be the death of the testator. For a testament is in force after men are dead, since it has no power at all while the testator lives. Therefore not even the first covenant was dedicated without blood" (Hebrews 9:16-18). After a covenant was ratified, it could not be altered.

Signs or altars worked like signatures would in a contract. It provided proof of an agreement. They needed witnesses to be enforced. "One witness shall not rise against a man concerning any iniquity or any sin that he commits; by the mouth of two or three witnesses the matter shall be established" (Deuteronomy 19:15; & Proverbs 2:17; Malachi 2:14; Joshua 9:20).

Contract versus Covenant

Unilateral contract is a one-sided agreement. The offeror can make a specific offer to one person, group, or the general public. The offeree accepts by completing a task (or refraining from a specific action). Example: "If you paint my fence, I (promise) to pay you $100." Bilateral contract is a two-sided agreement. They both agree to be bound. Example: "If you (promise) to paint my fence, I (promise) to pay you $100."[17] The offeree must manifest an objective willingness to accept.

- *Bilateral Contract = Promise for Promise*
- *Unilateral Contract = Promise for Performance*

---

[17] Mikaloff Justine, "Unilateral Contract," LegalMatch, LegalMatch Legal Writer, accessed March 18, 2021, https://www.legal-match.com/law-library/article/unilateral-contracts.html.

"If you paint my fence, I promise to pay you $100." In this unilateral example, the offeree is not obligated to paint the fence. If the offeree starts to paint the fence (performing), it shows an attempt to accept the offer is at hand, and the offeror should give the offeree sufficient time to complete the task. After the offeree starts performing (except for reward-type contracts), the offer becomes irrevocable. Some courts believe the contract was never accepted if rescinded by the offeror, or if the offeree did not complete the performance. The general rule of thumb is, after the offeree starts to perform, all parties are bound to their agreed upon performances.[18] After the performance is completed, the promise becomes *unconditional*.[19]

Covenants are for life. Covenants are a permanent change of status or relationship. In a unilateral contract, the offeree's completion of the performance is the acceptance. In a unilateral covenant, since the performance is on-going and cannot be completed, a small token (act) of acceptance is required. The offeree completes an unrelated task or act (sign/symbol). Unrelated so it would not be understood as the performance. Contracts could morph from one form to another. It is possible for a contract to start unilateral then morph bilaterally. Same with bilateral contracts. Long-term unilateral contracts morph bilaterally after the offeree starts performing, such as painting a house or building a barn.[20] Bilateral contracts morph unilat-

---

[18] "The courts have held that, as soon as a promisee has begun to perform or provide under the unilaterally offered contract, it becomes bilateral, with both parties bound to certain performance." see Legal Dictionary, "Bilateral Contract," by Content Team, accessed March 18, 2021, https://legaldictionary.net/bilateral-contract/.

[19] Encyclopedia.com, "Unilateral Contract," Reference West's Encyclopedia of American Law, Copyright 2005, The Gale Group, Inc., accessed April 15, 2021, http://www.encyclopedia.com/law/encyclopedias-almanacs-transcripts-and-maps/unilateral-contract.

[20] "Suppose you promise to pay someone $500 to paint your house. The promise sounds like an offer to enter a unilateral contract that binds

erally after the offeree completes the performance but the offeror still has on-going obligations.[21] The husband and wife were betrothed (covenanted) after drinking the cup of wine. Although betrothed (married by all intents and purposes), the marriage is not complete until the man takes possession of his wife in consummation. Contracts call it *consummation of sale.*

In a marriage covenant, the cup of wine is the acceptance that made (cut) the covenant, and becoming one-flesh is the performance required by the offeree to complete the marriage (Genesis 2:24). God's covenant with Abraham, circumcision is the acceptance that made (cut) the covenant, and faith is the performance required by the offeree for salvation. God's covenant with Moses, circumcision is the acceptance that made (cut) the covenant, and works (obeying the Law of Moses) is the performance required by the offeree for salvation. God's covenant with us through His Son, Jesus, baptism was the acceptance that made (cut) the covenant (we were baptized into Jesus's death for He shed His blood for us), and faith was the performance required by us (offeree) for salvation. Just as faith is a one-time act and continuous requirement (walk in faith), the woman's sexual performance is one-time and continuous (Romans 7:3-4; 1 Corinthians 7:3-4). The man was permitted

---

only you until the promisee accepts by painting your house. But what constitutes lawful "performance" under these circumstances? The act of beginning to paint your house or completely finishing the job to your satisfaction? Most Courts would rule that the act of beginning performance under these circumstances converts a unilateral contract into a bilateral contract, requiring both parties to fulfill the obligations contemplated by the contract." See Law.jrank, "Bilateral Contract," accessed March 18, 2021, https://law.jrank.org/pages/4745/Bilateral-Contract.html.

[21] Central Adjustment Board v. Ingram (TN, 1984); issue of no-compete clauses signed after commencement of employment. "But after years of work at the company, the deficient bilateral contract morphs into unilateral contract because CAB performed (kept as employed)." Gillette, "Contracts. Which Promises Get Enforced?," accessed December 10, 2017, http://www.law.nyu.edu/sites/default/files/upload_documents/Gillette%5B1%5D.Contracts.Fall2005.2.doc.

14

to put away his wife for violating the one-flesh performance (Deuteronomy 24:1). Because of the bride price, the woman was to be sexually exclusive to her husband. When the man and woman made a covenant by drinking the cup of wine, they entered into a mutual agreement that offered both parties certain guarantees in the marriage. The man was bound by promise and the woman through acceptance (by drinking the wine, she accepted to be bound by covenant). If the father arranged his daughter's marriage (at a young age), the young woman was obligated in marriage because of her father's authority (consummation required). However, if the father permits his daughter to partake of the consideration process by allowing her to drink the wine, but she refuses, the agreement is null and void (lacking consideration) and the bride price is rejected.

- *Offer = Proposal*
- *Acceptance = Assent*
- *Consideration = Mutual Benefit*

Contracts have three main elements: offer, acceptance, and consideration. The offeror is master of the offer and dictates how an offer is accepted. Consideration is the bargaining for exchange (payment) and meeting of the minds (agreement). Consideration is the main element of a contract. Nondisclosure, misrepresentation, duress, and undue influence compromises genuine assent and makes a contract voidable. Duress is the unlawful coercion to intimidate a weaker party to contract.

Gifts are voluntary transfers of property. Gifts lack mutual benefit (*exchange of value*) needed to form a binding contract. This is the consideration of the contract. Exchange of value is money or any desired action or outcome. When a unilateral covenant performs as a gift, there is no acceptance required from the offeree because the offeree is not required to perform for the promise (*no performance*). Since the offeree does not perform, the offeror provided the witness (sign/symbol), "'The rainbow shall be in the cloud, and I will look on it to remember the everlasting covenant between God and every living creature of all flesh that is on the earth.' And God said to Noah, 'This is the sign of the covenant which I have established between Me and all flesh that is on the earth'" (Genesis 9:16-17).

- *Unilateral Covenant + Mutual Benefit = Offeree sign*
- *Unilateral Covenant – Mutual Benefit = Offeror sign*

If promised to receive a donut when you went to church, that would be an example of a unilateral promise. You are not obligated to attend, but promised to receive a donut if you do. Gym memberships are bilateral. You are not obligated to go to the gym, but you are obligated to pay every month until you cancel your membership. Although you can cancel anytime, you must give proper notice at the beginning of the month. Unilateral covenants promise blessings. Unilateral covenants offer blessings because the offeree is not obligated to perform by promise (*promise for performance*). If the offeree doesn't perform, they temporarily forfeit the blessing. However, if the offeree stops performing, the covenant is materially breached. A material breach, after a cure period, becomes a total breach. The offeree, technically, could be cut-off for a total breach. Bilateral covenants have both blessings and curses because the offeree is bound by promises and there is a penalty for a breach of promise (*promise for promise*). Curses were for partial and material breaches, but they could be cut off for a total breach. There are different types of treaties in the ancient Near East. The royal grant was a unilateral gift of land. The parity treaty was a treaty between two equal powers. The suzerain/vassal treaty was a treaty between a greater and weaker power. The Suzerain (ruler) would set the terms (blessings and curses), and the vassal (subordinate) would agree (by walking between the slain animals). The suzerain would also walk between the animals after the vassal. They would make a covenant to one another and to their god. The vassal pays the suzerain a tribute, promises fidelity, and promises to give soldiers in time of war.

The suzerain would guarantee protection and give land grants. However, only the vassal's promise was unilaterally enforced. The vassal would treat with one suzerain because it could be subordinate to only one ruler (suzerain could treat with many vassals). Similar to what we see in marriage. Suzerain/vassal treaties resembled adhesion contracts (boilerplate contracts). The lopsided suzerain/vassal treaty is bilateral in form but unilateral in obligation (weaker party had no bargaining power). Contracts are void if they lack an exchange of value, and voidable if the offeree was forced to sign under duress. Covenants, however, can't be voided because they were ratified in blood.

In a unilateral contract, if the offeree completes their performance, they are no longer obligated to continue performing. Stopping the performance would not be a *breach of contract*. Insurance contracts are unilateral and conditional.[22] The insurance company accepts the offer from the insured (application and first payment). The insurer promises coverage as long as the offeree pays the premium. However, the insurer can revoke coverage if the insured stops paying or doesn't meet certain conditions (reporting in timely manner).[23] Bilateral contracts have opt-out options.[24] However, these clauses must be in

---

[22] "However, insurance contracts are unilateral contracts, where only the insurer makes a legally enforceable promise to pay for covered losses. The company cannot sue the insured for breach of contract. However, insurance contracts are also conditional contracts – if the insured fails to pay the premium, or fails to abide by the contract, then the insurer is not obligated to pay for any of the insured's losses." see Thismatter.com, "Insurance Contracts: Consideration, Unilateral Contracts (conditional contracts)," William C. Spaulding, accessed September 25, 2017, http://thismatter.com/money/insurance/insurance-contracts.htm.

[23] Hu Sanhe, "Chapter 3. Legal Concepts of the Insurance Contract," revision f89211cd, accessed March 18, 2021, https://life-and-health-insurance-license.readthedocs.io/Chapter3.%20Legal%20Concepts%20of%20the%20Insurance%20Contract/.

[24] A clause that permits signatories to a contract to opt out of a particular provision, or to terminate the contract early. see Collins, "Opt-out Clause," English Dictionary, accessed March 18, 2021,

good faith and not based on objective standards.[25] The general standard is, agreements must be kept (*pacta sunt servanda*).[26] God cut off Israel for breaking their covenant to Him and gave them over to the sword, pestilence, famine, and their enemies (Jeremiah 34:20). In a divorce, man is no longer the husband; and she his wife (Hosea 2:2). He cut her off from the promise.

- *Contract = Temporary (this for that)*
- *Covenant = Permanent (blood — for life)*

Jonathan offered David a (unilateral) gift of friendship.[27] Jonathan being the greater (King's son) and David the lesser (shepherd having no bargaining power). "Therefore you shall deal kindly with your servant, for you have brought your servant into a *covenant* of the Lord with you." (1 Samuel 20:8). Their mutual friendship was a change of status or relationship. The same lopsided covenant in marriage. The man and woman are husband and wife (change of status) and were mutually (bilaterally) promised to each other and God as their witness. But only the wife is obligated (unilaterally) to be submissive

---

https://www.collinsdictionary.com/us/dictionary/english/opt-out-clause.

[25] "In effect, marriage lost whatever had distinguished it from cohabitation." see MacPherson, "Whose fault was no-fault divorce?," Ruth Institute, accessed August 31, 2019, http://www.ruthinstitute.org/ruth-speaks-out/whose-fault-was-no-fault-divorce.

[26] "[I]f the contract was freely signed between the parties, the pacta sung servanda rule prevails, as each of the parties must bear the responsibility assumed in the agreement of wills." see Soares & Machado, "Opt-Out Clause in Not a Bank Check under Good Faith Lens," Scientific Research, Scientific Research Publishing Inc., accessed April 29, 2024, https://www.scirp.org/journal/paperinformation?paperid=95332.

[27] Jonathan made (cut) a covenant with David. Jonathan the greater party (King's son) offered David the lesser party (Shepard) his robe, armor, sword, bow, and belt as a sign of a unilateral covenant. The act of acceptance and honor was to take it. Johnathan was obligated through promise (offeror). David was obligated through acceptance (offeree). Jonathan's one-sided gift ratified the covenant (*lopsided performance*).

and sexually exclusive to her husband by Moses for divorce. Man (baal/master), "Yet you say, 'For what reason?' Because the Lord has been witness between you and the wife of your youth, with whom you have dealt treacherously; yet she is your companion and your wife by *covenant*" (Malachi 2:14). Woman (subordinate), "Who forsakes the companion of her youth, and forgets the *covenant* of her God?" (Proverbs 2:17).

- *Bride Price = Purchase Price*
- *Ketubah = Promise for Performance*
- *Wine = Act of Acceptance*
- *Consummation = Latin verb: To sum up or finish.*

Kings unilaterally gave daughters as rewards, "Here is my older daughter Merab; I will give her to you as a wife. Only be valiant for me, and fight the Lord's battles." (1 Samuel 18:17-18). And, "He who attacks Kirjath Sepher and takes it, to him I will give Achsah my daughter as a wife." (Joshua 15:16-17).

How God Sees a Covenant

God made a unilateral covenant with Abraham and his Seed (Genesis 15). We know it is unilateral because God was the *only* one who passed between the slain animals. Abraham did not make a reciprocal promise. However, he was asked to give a sign of the acceptance of the covenant by circumcision (*promise for performance*). "This is My covenant which you shall keep, between Me and you and your descendants after you: Every male child among you shall be circumcised... it shall be a sign of the covenant between Me and you." The un-circumcised man violated God's covenant (Genesis 17:14).[28]

---

[28] The offer is proof of willingness to be bound – A reasonable person would think responding in a certain way (by accepting the offer or performing a requested act) will create a contract. see Harris & Samuel, "Business Law Basics, Chapter 18: Contract Law. 18.2 Contract Formation," accessed January 17, 2019, http://www.businesslawbasics.com/chapter-18-contract-law.

When an offeror requests an act in return for his promise, the performance creates sufficient acceptance of the agreement.[29]

God's covenant to Abraham was conditional in form but not in substance.[30] The covenant has elements of a conditional covenant but its primarily unconditional. As long as Abraham remained in faith, he was guaranteed to receive the promise. Since God required a performance for the promise, it is a this-for-that agreement (*exchange of value*). Circumcision was not the (item of value) performance that made Abraham righteous. Circumcision was only the sign/symbol of his righteousness. Abraham believed and his faith was credited as righteousness (Romans 4:3). Abraham was justified by faith, not works, and faith without works is dead (Romans 4:2). For faith is not a performance in the traditional sense of the word since it has no tangible value in itself (*exchange of value*). Therefore, we are saved by faith and works (James 2:24). God tested his faith to see if it was steadfast and genuine. James calls the testing of his faith a work (James 2:21). "Was not Abraham our father justified by works when he offered Isaac his son on the altar?"

Moses' covenant grew old and was ready to vanish away (Jeremiah 31:31; Hebrews 8:13). God made a covenant with Moses and the people. The leaders of Israel walked between the slain animals (as representatives), and all the people promised to obey the laws given by Moses. Moses' covenant was bilateral: promise by God (blessings and cursing) and promise by the people. "Then he took the Book of the Covenant and read in the hearing of the people. They said, 'All that the Lord has said we will do, and be obedient" (Exodus 24:7). Moses

---

[29] Quimbee, "Acceptance by Performance," accessed March 18, 2021, https://www.quimbee.com/keyterms/acceptance-by-performance.

[30] "…Conditional in form but not in substance." see National Paralegal College, "Termination of the Power of Acceptance," (4) A qualified or conditional acceptance by the offeree, accessed January 30, 2017, https://nationalparalegal.edu/public_documents/courseware_asp_files/contracts/MutualAssentOfferAndAcceptance/TerminationAcceptance.asp.

sprinkled the blood on the people of Israel and the book of the law ratifying the covenant. (Jesus sprinkles us with his blood). Covenants that require something of value from the offeree are *quid pro quo* (this for that) and need a sign (circumcision) to show they are willing to contract. Moses' promise, righteousness is conditional on works of the law (*promise for promise*). They were cursed if they did not obey all the works of the law.

- *Promise of Works = Salvation is by works of the Law*
- *Performance of Faith = Salvation is by faith in Jesus*

Then versus Now

"Moses, because of the hardness of your hearts, permitted you to divorce your wives..." (Matthew 19:8). Divorce was not designed, "but from the beginning [divorce] was not so." Moses allowed man to put away his wife because sin increased in the giving of the Law (Romans 7:8). The cup of acceptance displayed the woman's willingness to enter into a covenant. Drinking the wine was not a performance (exchange of value). It was a minor act of acceptance (similar to signing a contract). The performance (item of value) was the woman becoming exclusively one flesh with her husband to produce children. Wine was the sign/symbol of the covenant (act of acceptance). The woman became one and that is why virginity was valued. After she completed her performance (consummation), man's promise to be her husband became unconditional. But Moses put a conditional clause in the covenant that allowed man to put away his wife (Deuteronomy 24:1). The wife was required to be faithful to her husband and to fill the earth with his seed. If he became jealous and felt his wife was unfaithful, he would bring her to the priest, and she would drink the bitter waters of remembrance that brings a curse (holy water and dust from the floor of the tabernacle).[31] If she were pregnant and unfaithful, she would not conceive. Her belly would swell and thighs rot.

---

[31] This was to protect the man's heritage (Numbers 5:26-27; Hosea 1:2).

The wedding band is a crucial part of the marriage ceremony.[32] Jewish law allowed the woman to accept the wedding ring as the bride price. It was based on Abraham's servant giving precious things to Rebekah. "Then the servant brought out jewelry of silver, jewelry of gold, and clothing and gave them to Rebekah. He also gave precious things to her brother and to her mother" (Genesis 24:53). The belief is women are acquired through money (something of value), document, or sexual intercourse.[33] That is why his marriage proposal says, "With this (item of value) ring, you are consecrated to me according to the law of Moses and Israel." However, the bride price was intended to establish transfer of authority from one to another. Rebecca's father refused the payment and gave his daughter to Abraham's servant to be Isaac's wife. Precious things were a gift rather than a payment. Therefore, the Jews got this wrong. This was likely influenced by social pressure. Bride price contractually establishes man's *rule* over his wife (Genesis 3:16).

"Or do you not know, brethren (for I speak to those who know the law), that the law has dominion over a man as long as he lives? For the woman who has a husband is bound by the law to her husband as long as he lives. But if the husband dies, she is released from the law of her husband. So then, if, while *her* husband lives, she marries another man, she will be called an adulteress; but if her husband dies, she is free from that law, so that she is no adulteress, though she has married another man" (Romans 7:1-4).

The widow was required to be the wife of only one man to partake of the widow's fund in the Church (1 Timothy 5:9). She was bound to the law of her husband as long as he lived

---

[32] Lamm, "The Marriage Ring," accessed May 26, 2018, https://www.chabad.org/library/article_cdo/aid/481776/jewish/The-Marriage-Ring.htm.
[33] Mishnah – Kiddusin 1:1.

(Romans 7:2-5). If a woman remarried while her husband still lived, she would not qualify for financial help from the church. The fund was set aside for the woman who lived a moral and upright life and helped raise children. Since it was not immoral for a widow to remarry, if the widow did remarry and her second husband died, she would still be eligible to receive funds. Paul did not feel a need to explain this assumption. Polygamy was not unlawful, and had a function in scripture (Genesis 29; Deuteronomy 21:15; 1 Kings 11:3; Jeremiah 3:8).[34] "And in that day seven women shall take hold of one man, saying, 'We will eat our own food and wear our own apparel; only let us be called by your name, to take away our reproach'" (Isaiah 4:1).

Church leaders (Overseers and Deacons) were required to be the husband of only one wife (1 Timothy 3:2, 12; Titus 1:6). Kings and Priests had strict requirements for marriage because of their position of leadership (Example: Moses did not enter the Promised Land because he misrepresented God). Priests did not partake in polygamy according to Jewish tradition. They married virgins or widow of a priest (Leviticus 21:7, 14). They were not to marry divorced women, regular widows, or defiled women. Kings were not to multiply their horses, gold, or wives (Jewish tradition said no more than 3 x 6 = 18).[35] The husband of one wife and the wife of one husband was first on the list of qualifications. Paul appeared to want to hold leaders and widows to the same standard in marriage and divorce.[36]

---

[34] Weiss, "Divorce: The Halakhic Perspective: Dispensation to Take a Second Wife."

[35] Deuteronomy 17:17.

[36] To understand 1 Tim. 3:2, 12 we look at 1 Tim. 5:9. Timothy and Titus were letters to the churches in Greece. In Greece, a woman's divorce had to be initiated by a male or male representative (by the husband, the archon (a city official), or her father or brother). Gentiles did not marry in polygamy, but Jews did during the Hellenistic period. 1 Timothy 3:11-12 and Titus 1:6 gives us a hint it had to do with a man's family life. Paul wanted men to show leadership in his family before being appointed as a leader of the church. The remarried man did not have his wife and house (children) in order, could have a bad reputation with

23

Polygamy was practiced only by Jews in Greece and Palestine at this time but not by surrounding Nations (other than rulers). Polygamy was not addressed as a sin in the New Testament, so the husband of one wife was not addressing polygamy but divorce and remarriage. (But unlawful in Greece and Rome).[37]

The Gospel Accounts of Divorce

I am sure the Pharisees would have heard what Jesus said about divorce to the multitudes (Matthew 5:32). Jesus did not address men who put away their wife. This was a hot topic for the religious leaders. Jesus says, "And I say to you," as He did on the Sermon on the Mount and Mark 10:11 (Matthew 19:9). Jesus spoke to His disciples in private at home (Mark 10:10). Jesus stays consistent with his message and says, whoever puts away his wife unlawfully and remarries commits adultery. He broadens the meaning of adultery from a man having relations with a married woman to a man unlawfully divorcing his wife and remarrying. And the men who married these women. Jesus also broadens sexual sin (fornication/sexual immorality), forbidding relationships with concubines and unmarried women (Hebrews 13:4; 1 Corinthians 6:18). Revolutionizing adultery.

Matthew must be interpreted in light of the other Gospels (Mark 10:10-11; Luke 16:18). Jesus shocks the conscience with those who justified themselves (strain at a gnat but swallowed a camel). It's a judgement that extended beyond the interpretation of the law to the heart. Anger is murder and lust is

---

those outside the church, and could fall into the reproach and snare of the devil. 1 Tim. 3:2, *"to be (present infinitive, ongoing or consecutive) one wife husband."* 1 Tim. 5:9, *"has been (a feminine participle of the verb "to be") one husband wife."* This was more about faithfulness in marriage and being above reproach, not polygamy (woman at the well).

[37] "Despite their official condemnation of polygamy, many respectable Romans had multiple marriages because divorce was easily obtained, and mistresses were openly accepted." see David Instone-Brewer, "Does Jesus Contradict the Old Testament on Polygamy?," accessed March 18, 2021, https://blog.logos.com/does-jesus-contradict-the-old-testament-on-polygamy/.

adultery (heart), yes be yes (integrity), turn cheek (response), love enemies (in action), and be perfect as God (in everything).

Jesus said a man would cause his wife to commit adultery if he did not put her away for sexual immorality (porniea).[38] Since Jewish men were divorcing a wife based on the religious leader's understanding of the law (*any reason*), we can safely assume men were marrying these unlawfully divorced women.

Mark does not mention the *any reason* clause of the Jews. This is probably why the exception clause is not mentioned. Mark addressed Jews living in Rome. This probably why Mark mentioned woman-initiated divorces (Mark 10:12). Pharisees would not have allowed a woman to put away her husband or for her to marry again without a get (writ) of divorce from him.

Mark hinted of an exemption clause when it said, a man commits adultery against his wife if he divorces and remarries (Mark 10:11). *Against her* suggests she was not lawfully put away (Deuteronomy 24:1). In the Old Testament, Priests put away their wife to marry young, pagan women (Malachi 2:11).

"He who marries [the/a] put away woman commits adultery" (Matthew 5:32). Without a definite article, we must use context to understand this passage. Was it adultery to marry *a* divorced woman or to marry *the* divorced woman? Luke says, he who marries *any* woman who was put away from a husband commits adultery (Luke 16:18). The key to understanding this passage is the word *adultery*. You can't commit adultery without marriage. The same ambiguity was seen in Matthew 5:28. Jesus says, if a man lusts after a woman, he commits adultery in his heart. The Septuagint (Greek translation of the OT) translates the word lusts as *covet* (Exodus 20:17; Deuteronomy 5:21). We see *covet* used in other places (Romans 7:7, 13:9). This could suggest the man is not to *covet* another man's wife. Job made a covenant with eyes not to look at a woman in lust (Job 31:1). I believe Jesus was trying to use the understanding of adultery to shock the conscience of unfaithful husbands

---

[38] Matthew 19:9 is most likely the expanded account of Mark 10:10-12.

(Jeremiah 3:20). It was adultery for an unmarried man to have sexual relations with a married woman (Leviticus 18:20). However, it was not adultery for a married man to have sexual relations with an unmarried woman even at this time with Greece and Rome. Jesus admonished Jews for violating the Ten Commandments (do not murder, commit adultery, covet your neighbor's wife). Most all ancient civilizations did not consider it adultery for married men to have sexual relations with unmarried women (Rome, Greece, Code of Hammurabi). At times, even modern civilizations (England, United States). Adultery had to do with theft of another man's reproductive and property rights over his wife. The point of the *but I say to you* was to expand the letter of the law to the spirit of the law. Jesus admonished men who lusted after women unlawfully, divorced unlawfully, or married unlawfully divorced women. According to Jesus, an unlawful divorce was no divorce at all.

The Letter to the Corinthians

10. Now to the married I command, yet not I but the Lord: A wife is not to depart from her husband. 11. But even if she does depart, let her remain unmarried or to be reconciled to her husband. And a husband is not to divorce his wife. 12. But to the rest I, not the Lord, say: If any brother has a wife who does not believe, and she is willing to live with him, let him not divorce her. 13. And a woman who has a husband who does not believe, if he is willing to live with her, let her not divorce him. 14. For the unbelieving husband is sanctified by the wife, and the unbelieving wife is sanctified by the husband; otherwise your children would be unclean, but now they are holy. 15. But if the unbeliever departs, let him depart; a brother or a sister is not under bondage in such cases. But God has called us to peace. 16. For how do you know, O wife, whether you will save your husband? Or how do you know, O husband, whether you will save your wife? – 1 Corinthians 7:10-16

The woman at the well (John 4:18; 1 Corinthians 14:24). Being shunned and forced to draw water in the heat of the day, Jesus admonished the Samaritan for being married five times. We see it was an admonishment because fornication is also on the list of sins. The reason for the divorces were not important.

"...and let not the husband *put away* [emphasis added] his wife" (1 Corinthians 7:11b, KJV).

The word *separate* or *depart* is used to describe divorce. Separate tells what divorce did. It separated what God joined together. Gentiles used *separate* in their divorce documents. Josephus uses the word *diachwrizw* as departs (similar in emphasis to *chwrizw*) in the *Antiquities of the Jews*. Depart seems describe a generic term for divorce like separate. 1 Corinthians 7:11b and 12-13 used *aphienai* for divorce (similar in emphasis *ephiémi)* however, this word appeared to be used by Paul to describe divorce by reason. Some Bibles translate *aphienai* as put away[39] or send away.[40] Divorce (*aphienai*) is similar in emphasis to put away (*ephiémi*) that Josephus used when speaking of an additional step in the Jewish divorce process.[41]

- "But some time afterward, when Salome happened to quarrel with Costobarus; she sent him a document and dissolved (*apolumené* from *apoluw*) her marriage with him, though this was not according to the Jewish laws;

---

[39] Herodotus 5:39.
[40] Bible Hub Thayer's Greek Lexicon, STRONGS NT 863: ἀφίημι. Section 1, To send away, accessed April 18, 2018, http://biblehub.com/greek/863.htm.
[41] David Instone-Brewer believes *aphienai* cannot refer to a proper Jewish divorce. See David Instone-Brewer, "1 Corinthians 7 in the Light of the Graeco-Roman Marriage and Divorce Papyri," Tyndale Bulletin pp.106-107, accessed April 29, 2024, https://tyndalebulletin.org/api/v1/articles/30262-1-corinthians-7-in-the-light-of-the-graeco-roman-marriage-and-divorce-papyri.pdf.

for with us it is lawful for a husband to do so; but a wife, if she departs (*diachwristheisé* from *diachwrizw*) from her husband, cannot of herself be married to another, unless her former husband put her away (*ephientos* from *ephiémi*)"[42] (Antiquities of the Jews 15:259).

- "Therefore what God has joined together, let not man separate (*chwrizetw* from *chwrizw*)" (Matthew 19:6).

- "And I say to you, whoever divorces (*apolusé* from *apoluw*[43]) his wife, except for sexual immorality, and marries another commits adultery" (Matthew 19:9a).

- "Now to the married I command, yet not I but the Lord: A wife is not to depart (*chwristhénai* from *chwrizw*) from her husband. But even if she does depart (*chwristhé* from *chwrizw*), let her remain unmarried or be reconciled to her husband. And a husband is not to divorce (*aphienai*) his wife" (1 Corinthians 7:10-11).

Ezra 10:3 versus 1 Corinthians 7:14

"Now therefore, let us make a covenant with our God to put away all these wives and those who have been born to them, according to the advice of my master and of those who tremble at the commandment of our God; and let it be done according to the law" (Ezra 10:3, the law of Ezra).

"For the unbelieving husband is sanctified by the wife, and the unbelieving wife is sanctified by the husband; otherwise your children would be unclean, but now they are holy" (1 Corinthians 7:14).

---

[42] Instone-Brewer, "1 Corinthians 7 in the Light of the Graeco-Roman Marriage and Divorce Papyri," 107.

[43] David Instone-Brewer believes this to be apoluw. Dr. habil. Christian A. Eberhart said this is apoluo.

The Corinthians thought they were commanded (by law) to put away their unbelieving spouse because unbelievers were unclean, practicing pagan worship (Ezra 10:3). We can come to this conclusion because Paul said the children would have been unclean (same as the spouse) if not for the sanctification of the unbeliever. The law commanded men to separate from the Nations they came to occupy (wife and children) and put them away. "The people of Israel and the priests and the Levites have not separated themselves from the peoples of the lands... For they have taken some of their daughters as wives for themselves and their sons, so that the holy seed is mixed with the peoples of those lands" (Ezra 9:1-2). Believers were told not be unequally yoked with unbelievers (2 Corinthians 6:17; a reference to Isaiah 52:11 "do not touch what is *unclean...*"). Sanctified does not mean saved, it means set apart, It's the Holy Spirit in believers that sanctifies the unbeliever.[44]

Paul lays some groundwork before he answers questions about divorce and remarriage, "Now concerning the things of which you wrote me" (1 Corinthians 7:1). The church asked him to relay commands from the Lord (1 Corinthians 7:25, 9:14, 14:37). The Gospel message came through the revelation of Jesus Christ (Galatians 1:11-12). Paul repeated commands from the Lord ("Lord says, not I"), but not about virgins or unbelievers (1 Corinthians 7:12 "I, not the Lord, say," 25). Paul tells them that the Lord hates divorce, and not to separate what God has joined together (Malachi 2:4-6; Matthew 19:6).

When we are *overcome* by someone or something greater than ourselves, we have been brought into captivity (slavery). We are no longer free but slaves (2 Peter 2:19). Believers obedient to the letter of the law are under *bondage* (enslavement). "But now after you have known God, or rather are known by God, how is it that you turn again to the weak and beggarly

---

[44] The Holy Spirit cannot be defiled. Paul demonstrates that unbelievers are sanctified because of the union between the two and sharing a vestige of sprit (Malachi 2:15). The unbeliever loses sanctification after a divorce, but the children remain holy because they were born that way.

elements, to which you desire again to be in bondage?" (Galatians 4:9). We are not to be entangled again with a yoke of bondage (Galatians 5:1). Creation itself will someday be *set free* from the *bondage* of decay (Romans 8:21). Believers are not bound by law, command, or moral responsibility to stay married to save their unbelieving spouse (1 Corinthians 7:16).

Paul said believers are *bound* to our spouse when married (1 Corinthians 7:27, 39). But also says, believers are not under bondage if the unbeliever separates (1 Corinthians 7:15). But what did he mean? Some believe *bondage* refers to the covenant of marriage. But it can't. *Bondage* is used in the perfect tense which communicates a completed act that has present-day implications. Paul is referring to the fact (completed act) that we died to the law (Galatians 2:19). And the fact (present day implication) that all things are lawful (1 Corinthians 6:12). Paul is saying, we are not enslaved to the law to stay married.

Bondage is slightly different than bound. Though these words are similar and can be used interchangeably at times. We see bound used in both a positive and negative sense in scripture. *Bound* meant tied and *loosed* untied. These words were used as opposites. Example: shoelaces can be tied or untied. Bound and loosed were common phrases used by the Jews in different situations. Someone could be bound by their oath, promise, or duty to do something (take care of widow). One can be bound or loosed in sickness (Luke 13:16). Bondage, however, had a negative expression that meant enslavement. Although words like free, loosed, and liberty were used to express someone who is no longer bound or under bondage. Bound could be used to express the commitment in marriage (i.e. marriage bond). Bondage would not be used for marriage.

Paul said, the Lord commands a woman not to separate from her husband (1 Corinthians 7:10). This was likely said to address woman married to unbelievers (1 Corinthians 7:13). Women thought they were to "put away" the unclean husband. If divorce was lawful, they assumed remarriage was lawful. Paul wanted to be clear the general rule is men and women are not to divorce one another (1 Corinthians 7:10-11). Paul said, a woman is not to separate from her husband, but if separated, she *must* (command in the Greek) remain unmarried or *must* reconcile to her husband. But why did Paul give women the option to remain unmarried before reconciliation? Jesus might have hinted of reconciliation of the man who put away his wife without knowledge of any sexual immorality (Matthew 5:32). Paul's message in this chapter is to *remain* in the situation they are called into (1 Corinthians 7:8, 11, 20, 24, and 40). Paul is saying, women are not to initiate the separation, however, if the unbeliever is the one who separates from the marriage, they *must* (passive imperative) let them, "let them separate." Paul gives believers (brother/sister) permission to divorce in these types of situations (cases). Paul does not give them permission to remarry, therefore, since the divorce was unlawful (separated), remarriage at this time would be unlawful. Paul was giving this command, not the Lord, so Paul will be limited in his scope of authority. When instruction is silent, we are to assume to turn to the law. Instead of specifically giving believers permission to remarry, he tells them to walk in the situation (calling) they are in, now they are saved (1 Corinthians 7:17).

Paul said, when someone is past the flower of their youth (this is when a flower begins to fade) and desires to marry, that the Church should allow this group of people to get married, "let them marry" (*unmarrieds* vs. 8, 36). These were believers that were spoken about earlier who were burning with passion. Virgin in these following passages could mean men or women (Revelations 14:4). It could be speaking of his own virginity, and not about a daughter or a man who is betrothed to a virgin.

Corinthians appear to be divided. Some thought they were to leave their unbelieving spouse, obeying the law (Ezra 10:3). Others thought they were to stay married to their unbelieving spouse since there was no sexual immorality in the marriage, obeying the law (Deuteronomy 24:1). But Paul says something unexpected. If the unbeliever is willing to remain married, "let them remain (do not divorce)," but if they separate, "let them separate (do divorce)." He is giving a possible future scenario. *If* this happens, *then* you are not under bondage in such *cases*. "For wherever you go, I will go; and wherever you lodge, I will lodge" (Ruth 1:16). Since Paul is giving this command (I say, not the Lord) he is going to give biblical principles for his instructions. Do not divorce the unbelieving spouse for being unclean because the Holy Spirit in you sanctified your spouse. This question pulls at their heart strings because if the unbeliever needed to be put away, so would their unclean children. Paul assures them the children are holy (1 Corinthians 7:14). Next, he reasons with them why they are not required to stay married though Jesus commanded believers not to separate (Matthew 19:6; 1 Corinthians 7:10-11) and lacking support (Deuteronomy 24:1). God called you to live in peace with the unbeliever (1 Corinthians 7:15). This whole chapter is about not fighting against the will of the unbeliever. You are not required, under bondage to the biblical requirements in the law, to remain married. It is reasonable to assume some thought if the law commanded them to divorce their unbelieving spouse, then remarriage would have been lawful (1 Corinthians 7:15). By Paul using the words *under bondage* and *separate* we can conclude he is saying this is not a lawfully sanctioned divorce. Remarriage must be approved by law (1 Corinthians 7:11, 27). The word *called* connected this to slavery and circumcision. We are to remain content where we find ourselves when saved. Slave, free, circumcised, or uncircumcised. Like marriage. Married, single, divorced, or widowed. The wife is bound by law ("as the law also says") as long as her husband lives; but if her husband dies [*sleeps*], she is free to remarry, in the Lord.

Law of the Husband

> "Indeed you are called a Jew and rest on the law, and make your boast in God... you who make your boast in the law, do you dishonor God through breaking the law?" – (Romans 2:17, 23).

"Or do you not know, brethren (for I speak to those who know the law), that the law has dominion [lords] over a man as long as he lives. For the woman who has a husband is bound by the law to her husband as long as he lives. But if the husband dies, she is released from the law of her husband" – Romans 7:1-2 (and 1 Corinthians 7:39).

The definition of *law* is a rule of conduct that is enforced by a controlling agency. The law ensures proper moral and civil behavior (Romans 13:1-4). Scripture says, government praises you when you do good, but punishes you for evil. When you submit yourself to a governing authority, you submit yourself to its rules and guidelines. The term *law of* tells who is that controlling authority. As we might say, the *law of* the United States. We also use the term *law of* when speaking about the *law of* nature, *law of* gravity, and *the law* of physics.

Book of Romans, Paul uses the concept of law to the Jews when trying to make a point. The Jewish believers understood that law has dominion over you as long as you live. Paul includes a few other *laws* (rules and guidelines) set by the hand of God and known by the religious community. Like, "another law" (7:23), "law of the husband" (7:2-3), "law of sin" (7:23, 25), "law of God" (7:22), "law that evil is present with me" (7:21), "law of my mind" (7:23), "law of the Spirit" (Romans 8:2), "law of sin and death" (8:3), and the "law of faith" (3:26).

Paul studied under Gamaliel and was familiar with their ancestral laws. Laws the "law of jealousy" (Numbers 5:29), "law of burnt offering" (Leviticus 6:9), "law of grain offering" (6:14), "law of sin offering" (6:25), "law of the sacrifice of peace offerings" (7:11), "law of the burnt offering" (7:37), "law of leprous plague" (13:59), "law of the one who had a leprous sore" (14:32), and the "law of leprosy" (14:57). The law of the husband was a general term used by the Jews to describe the limitations of a woman being under the rule of her husband (Genesis 3:16). The man was not under the law of his wife because only she was said to be *under-man* (Romans 7:2).

"They say, 'If a man divorces his wife, and she goes from him and becomes another man's, may he return to her again? Would not that land be greatly polluted? But you have played the harlot with *many lovers*; Yet return to Me,' says the Lord." (Emphasis added) Jeremiah 3:1-10

Israel polluted herself by becoming one with many lovers. She was put away for her adulteries. Jeremiah 3:1 reference Deuteronomy 24:4. Israel defiled herself with stones and trees. Israel committed adultery with many lovers. The point of this passage was to show the great amount of sin the Lord is willing to forgiving but seek reconciliation of Israel. Hosea was called to marry a prostitute who had children in adultery to show God's relationship with Israel. Israel sold herself into sin and paid other men to make love to her (worse than a prostitute). He will buy them back and redeem (*Hebrew word is Padah*) (Isaiah 50:1-2; Ezekiel 16:31-34; Hosea 1:2-8, 2:2, 23, 3:1-2).

Spirit, Heart, and Holy

Jesus did not give man permission to put away his wife. Jesus only acknowledged the law allowed man to put away his wife for sexual immorality by not calling remarriage adultery. Those under the law cannot accomplish in their carnal minds (Romans 8:7) what we can accomplish in the Spirit having the mind of Christ obeying the *righteous* requirements in the law (Romans 8:4; 1 Corinthians 2:16). Moses understood men living under the law were not be able to forgive a wayward wife.

God has given us a new heart (Ezekiel 36:26). Sin hardens the heart (Hebrews 3:13). Paul tells husbands not to be bitter towards their wife but to love her as Christ loved the Church. Jesus said we are to forgive seventy times seven. If we do not forgive a repentant wife who seeks forgiveness, how will God forgive us since we have sinned so greatly against Him? "So My heavenly Father also will do to you [delivered to the torturers and repay] if each of you, from his heart, does not forgive his brother [or sister] his trespasses" (Matthew 18:21:35).

Men were using the law as an excuse to divorce their wife. Women were using civil law to separate from their husband. The Lord commanded women not to separate from their husband, and men not to divorce his wife (1 Corinthians 7:10-11). We died to the law so that we can walk in the newness of life. For the law brings death, but the spirit brings life and peace. Paul said, "If you are led by the Spirit, you are not under law" (Galatians 5:18). Paul warns us not to return back to the law. Cursed is everyone who does not continue in all things which are written in the book of the law, to do them (Galatians 3:10).

"Where is the certificate of your mother's divorce, whom I have put away? Or which of My creditors is it to whom I have sold you? For your iniquities you have sold yourselves, and for your transgressions your mother has been put away" (Isaiah 50:1-3). God did not abandon Israel, they abandoned Him, and by their own sin sold themselves back into slavery (similar to Gomer). Israel was put away for her transgressions. "Is God's hand too short to save?" God hates divorce because He made them one. After hearing what Jesus said about God's expectations, the disciples said, "If such is the case of the man and his wife, it is better not to marry." (Matthew 19:10). But Jesus responds, "He who is able to accept it, let him accept it".

Unlawful divorce leads to adultery (Matthew 5:31-32). Therefore, we are to address those in the Church seeking to divorce for unlawful reasons. We are to purge out sin least it defiles the whole church. "Therefore purge out the old leaven" (1 Corinthians 5:6). We are to rebuke in private, but if they do not listen, bring witnesses (Matthew 18:15). If they do not hear the witnesses, we are to take them to the elders. If they refuse to hear the church, they should be excommunicated and treated as heathens or tax collectors. Not to hate them as enemies, but to admonish them as brothers and sisters in Christ. "Deliver such a one to Satan for the destruction of the flesh that his spirit may be saved in the day of the Lord Jesus" (1 Corinthians 5:5).

Why should a woman be submissive to her husband if she was not acquired by a bride price? Adam was formed first then

Eve. Paul said, the order of creation gave man preference in leadership (1 Timothy 2:13). Man was not created for the woman, but the woman was created for the man. God's purpose has always been headship. It is not good for man to be alone, so God made man a helper that was comparable to him, but Eve was deceived by the serpent. The fall of woman and her ability to be deceived is another reason for male headship. Men should not take advantage of their physical strength but give honor to women as weaker vessels and co-heirs of heaven (1 Peter 3:7). Women should be obedient to their husband, as the law also says, so the Word of God is not blasphemed by the unbelievers (Genesis 3:16; 1 Corinthians 14:34; Titus 2:5).

God designed one man for one woman (Adam and Eve). Jews believe monogamy was God's design. We see one man for one woman in the animals being loaded on the ark and God creating one helper (Genesis 2:18). God did not want Kings to multiply their wives to keep their hearts from being led astray. Paul said man seeks the things of the world to please his wife. To serve the Lord without distraction, it is best not to marry. For a leader in the Church to be chosen they must have only married once (1 Timothy 3:2, 12, Titus 1:6). This prevented leaders from taking advantage of their position, displays good leadership, and holds them to the highest standard like priests.

Did God design polygamous or monogamous marriages? By designing unilateral marriage with a bride price, it allowed men to marry in polygamy, if needed, even though monogamy was intended. Polygamy helped thwart the devil's schemes. We see this when Jacob was deceived by Laban (representing the devil) and married Rachel and Leah. This was an archetype of God marrying Israel and Judah (they were split due to sin). Neither polygamous marriage was intended, but the only way to marry the loved (apple of his eye) was to marry the unloved. Though this, God divinely decreed the twelve tribes of Israel. You can practice monogamy with unilateral marriage, but you cannot practice polygamy with bilateral marriage. Monogamy is the ideal, but forcing monogamy is scripturally problematic.

Remarriage

Question: *If a man divorces his innocent wife, is **she** free to remarry?*
Bound: Matthew 5:31-32 says a man causes his wife to commit adultery if he put her away without first knowing if she committed sexual immorality in the marriage (supposing she will remarry). Jesus focused on the sin of man when speaking to the multitudes (Matthew 5:26). This does not mean woman is free to remarry. It simply means the man shares in his wife's adultery when she marries because his sin caused it to happen.

Question: *If a man divorces his innocent wife, is **he** free to remarry?*
Bound: Scripture says, a woman *defiles* herself if she commits adultery with another man (Numbers 5:13). It also says, a divorced woman *defiles* herself to her first husband after she marries another (Deuteronomy 24:4). It would be an abomination for the first husband to take her back (Deuteronomy 24:4). The law does not require a man to put away his adulterous wife, nor does the law prevent a man from reconciling to his former adulterous wife if she never remarried (Jeremiah 3:1). If a man divorces his innocent wife he should try to reconcile.

Question: *If a woman initiates the divorce, is her husband free to remarry?*
Bound/Loosed: Churches allowed men and women to divorce for adultery, abuse, or abandonment. But this is not scriptural. If the woman initiated a divorce, it prevented the man from handing his wife a writ of divorce and sending her out of the home. If the man or woman unlawfully initiates a divorce, and the woman did not commit sexual immorality in the marriage, they should reconcile. If his wife was unwilling to return, he should be long-suffering and wait until she has defiled herself with another man before he remarries. If the woman did not defile herself with another, she has not broken the covenant in

uncleanness (Deuteronomy 24:1). Paul said a man should be *loosed* from a wife before he marries (1 Corinthians 7:27-28).

Question: *If a woman divorces her husband for abandonment, abuse, or adultery can she remarry if her husband remarries?*
Bound: If the man committed adultery or sexual immorality in the marriage, or if the man divorced his wife unlawfully, she is still bound to her husband by covenant (the law of her husband). The husband does not have power to override the law and give his wife permission to remarry. Unless she was lawfully put away and given a certificate of divorce, she is still married by law and bound to her husband as long as he lives (1 Corinthians 7:39). Since the law allows polygamy, a man's wife is not *loosed* because he remarries. The law forbidding reconciliation of a former wife who remarried does not apply to the man (Deuteronomy 24:4). Jesus commanded divorced women to remain unmarried or reconcile if separated from a husband (1 Corinthians 7:11). An unlawfully divorced woman is called an *agunah* (chained woman). The divorced woman was not allowed to remarry without a get from her husband. If she did remarry, and had children, her child would be called *mamzer* (born of a forbidden relationship) Deuteronomy 23:2.

Question: *Can both get remarried if the woman was lawfully divorced by her husband for sexual immorality (fornication)?*
Loosed: If a woman was lawfully put away by her husband, the marriage covenant was terminated according to contractual and scriptural principles (Deuteronomy 24:1; Hosea 2:2). The key to understanding remarriage is adultery. Not that adultery frees you, but can you remarry without committing adultery? Scripture does not give sinners explicit permission to remarry, "He is not the God of the dead, but the God of the living" (Mark 12:27). Moses said, "[She] goes and becomes another man's wife" (Deuteronomy 24:2). Since only the priests were discouraged from marrying a divorced woman, it seems it was not a sin and allowed for a common man (Leviticus 21:7, 14).

Adultery in the Bible: Adultery means to break wedlock (OT) or pollute/defile (NT). Idolatry was equivalent to adultery to God because it violated the exclusive *oneness* commitment. "Marriage is honorable among all, and the bed undefiled; but fornicators and adulterers God will judge" (Hebrews 13:4). Adultery defiles and breaks the covenant in unfaithfulness (Jeremiah 31:32). Some of the Jews believed the bride price made the woman a type of possession. Therefore, adultery was stealing the reproductive and property rights of the husband. The man who also slept with a married woman was guilty of adultery. The exclusive sexual performance was a wife's duty in the Old Testament. The man had sexual expectations in the marriage (Exodus 21:10). In the New Testament, the husband and wife both had sexual duties, and their bodies belonged to each other (1 Corinthians 7:4). They were not to deny the other without mutual consent. If polygamy was lawful in the Old Testament, why would it be unlawful in the New Testament? Jesus met people where they were at and preach from there. Jesus appeared to use a parable about polygamy when He said, *ten virgins* took oil lamps to meet the bridegroom (Matthew 25:1). *Virgin* was code for bride. It seems that Jesus was trying not to overtly challenge their laws and culture. Jesus did not change the law, only the sexual expectations of the believer. Believers were commanded not to have sex before marriage, and sex should only be practiced in the confines of marriage (Hebrews 13:4). Jesus did not commend monogamy or polygamy, but for believers to be without reproach (1 Timothy 3:7). Remarriage of the man would not be *adultery* if polygamy was lawful. However, it was *adultery* for the man to unlawfully divorce his wife and remarry in a monogamous society since it violated the marriage covenant and prevented reconciliation. J. Fineman (2016) said, "If the woman does remarry [without a "get"], she is considered an adulteress... However, Jewish men who remarry without giving a "get" don't suffer the same consequences. Because traditional Jewish law permitted polygamy, these men are not considered adulterers..." (para. 8).

Acknowledgments

"If any of you lacks wisdom, let him ask of God, who gives to all liberally and without reproach, and it will be given to him" (James 1:5). Thank you, for helping me understand divorce. "Let God (our Father) be true, but every man a liar!" This message is for my daughter, Padah. Your father always tells you the truth, and everyone who says differently is a liar.

I want to thank Given O. Blakely for his YouTube video. Dr. David Instone-Brewer for his help. Dr. Christian Eberhart and Tim McMillian. Dr. Eberhart for his review. Thank you, all the professors who gave me your additional time and input. All testimonies were given by expressed written permission. Not all professors who gave testimony agreed with this book. I recently changed my understanding of husband of one wife.

Thank you, those who helped me with editing this book. Thank you, Stratton, for giving the title The Cure for Divorce. Thank you, Adam, for your wisdom when I came to you about the controversial gender passages, knowingly or unknowingly. Please forgive for citing quotes incorrectly and poor grammar.

I will never leave you or forsake you, my daughter Padah! I pray for you every day. As God took back his children, I will take you back. That way, as God said, where I am, there you may be also (John 14:3; Revelation 12:5). Mommy, come back home as a bird that has wandered from its nest (Jeremiah 3:14).

Glossary of Terms

Act of Acceptance – a specific act required for acceptance
Acceptance – taking or receiving something that is offered
Bilateral – involving both sides
Condition – a situation with respect to circumstances
Condition in form – termination of shape
Condition in substance – termination of body
Conditional – contains at least one clause or terms
Confirmation – the piece of evidence
Confirmed – validation or ratified
Consideration (legal) – both parties intended to perform
Consummation of Sale – (Latin) "to sum up" or "to finish"
Contract – a mutual agreement validated by law
Continued performance – ongoing work, act or deed
Covenant – a formal or ceremonial promise or agreement
Oath – a promise strengthened by an appeal
Offeree – a person who receives the offer
Offeror – a person who makes the offer
Performance – accomplishment of work, act, or deed
Promise – expressed assurance
Quid pro quo (Latin) – this for that
Representation – working on behalf of another
Requirement – expressed obligation or demand
Sign – an action that indicates a meaning
Unconditional – absolute
Unilateral – one-sided

(Glossary of Terms used primarily from Dictionary.com)

Bibliography

Bible Hub Thayer's Greek Lexicon. STRONGS NT 863: ἀφίημι. Section 1. To send away. Accessed April 18, 2018. http://biblehub.com/greek/863.htm.

Bercot. D.W. *A Dictionary of Early Christian Beliefs.* Peabody, Massachusetts: Hendrickson Publishers, Inc., 1998.

Berean Patriot. "Why "Lusting" in Matthew 5:27-28 Doesn't Make All Men Adulterers." Home. Faith Articles. October 5, 2018. Accessed April 15, 2024. https://www.bereanpatriot.com/why-lusting-in-matthew-527-28-doesnt-make-all-men-adulterers/

Bieber, Christy. J.D. "Leading Causes of Divorce: 43% Report Lack of Family Support." Forbes Advisor. Updated: August 15, 2023. Accessed April 29, 2024. https://www.forbes.com/advisor/legal/divorce/common-causes-divorce/

Bleich, David. "Kiddushei Ta'ut: Annulment as a Solution to the Agunah Problem. Tradition 90 (1998): 33"; originally from - Weiss Susan. "Divorce: The Halakhic Perspective. Jewish Women: A Comprehensive Historical Encyclopedia." Jewish Women's Archive. Accessed February 5, 2017. https://jwa.org/encyclopedia/article/divorce-halakhic-perspective.

Bunch, Caleb. "Genesis 15." Levittown Baptist Church. February 1, 2023. Category: Genesis. Accessed April 20, 2024. https://www.levittownbaptist.com/shepherding-notes/post/genesis-15#:~:text=This%20was%20a%20practice%20that,would%20be%20required%20to%20agree.

Christianity Today. "Wayne Grudem Tells Us Why He Changed His Divorce Position." By Morgan Lee. December 4, 2019. Accessed December 29, 2021. https://www.christianitytoday.com/ct/podcasts/quick-to-listen/wayne-grudem-divorce-abuse-complementarianism.html

Collins. "Opt-out Clause." English Dictionary. Accessed March 18, 2021. https://www.collinsdictionary.com/us/dictionary/english/opt-out-clause.

Constable, Thomas. DD. "Commentary on 1 Samuel 18." "Dr. Constable's Expository Notes." Unsure of original source and quote. "[Note: Laney, p. 61.]" Accessed November 7, 2022. https://www.studylight.org/commentaries/eng/dcc/1-samuel-18.html. 2012.

Department of Justice. "Selected Statistics on Canadian Families and Family Law: Second Edition." Canada. Accessed January 30, 2019. https://www.justice.gc.ca/eng/rp-pr/fl-lf/famil/stat2000/p4.html.

Dictionary.com. "Feminism." & "Egalitarian." Glossary of Terms. 2021 Dictionary.com, LLC. Accessed April 15, 2021. https://www.dictionary.com/.

Dunnell, M. B. *Minnesota digest: a digest of the decisions of the Supreme Court of the State of Minnesota covering Minnesota Reports, 1-109, Northwestern Reporter, 1-125.* Owatonna, MN: Minnesota Law Book Co. 1910. p. 376 (reference 1725).

Encyclopedia.com. "Unilateral Contract." Reference West's Encyclopedia of American Law. Copyright 2005. The Gale Group, Inc. Accessed April 15, 2021.

http://www.encyclopedia.com/law/encyclopedias-alma-nacs-transcripts-and-maps/unilateral-contract.

Fineman, Julie. "The Importance of a "Get": A Jewish Divorce." Accessed April 15, 2021. https://theodys-seyonline.com/jewish-divorce.

Gillette. C. "Contracts. Which Promises Get Enforced?" Accessed December 10, 2017. http://www.law.nyu.edu/sites/default/files/upload_documents/Gillette%5B1%5D.Contracts.Fall2005.2.doc.

Harris, B. & Samuel. D. "Business Law Basics, Chapter 18: Contract Law. 18.2 Contract Formation." Accessed January 17, 2019. http://www.businesslawbasics.com/chapter-18-contract-law.

Heidemann, A. "Unilateral v. Bilateral Contracts: What is the difference." JD Advising. Accessed March 18, 2021. https://www.youtube.com/watch?v=pR9tqwuHCE0&feature=youtu.be.

Hodge, C. *Romans the Crossway Classic Commentaries.* Hodge & McGrath & Packer. Wheaton, Illinois: Crossway Books.1993. p. 197.

Instone-Brewer, David. "1 Corinthians 7 in the Light of the Graeco-Roman Marriage and Divorce Papyri." Tyndale Bulletin pp.106-107. Accessed April 29, 2024. https://tyndalebulletin.org/api/v1/articles/30262-1-corinthians-7-in-the-light-of-the-graeco-roman-marriage-and-divorce-papyri.pdf

Instone-Brewer, David. *Antiquities of the Jews 15:259, Matt. 19, 1 Cor. 7.* Accessed December 2016. Personal correspondence. Used by permission.

Instone-Brewer, David. "Does Jesus Contradict the Old Testament on Polygamy?" Accessed March 18, 2021. https://blog.logos.com/does-jesus-contradict-the-old-testament-on-polygamy/.

Jewish Wedding Blog. "The Origins of the Ketubah." Accessed December 10, 2017. https://www.jewishwedding101.com/the-origins-of-the-ketubah/

Kuperberg, A. "Does Premarital Cohabitation Raise Your Risk of Divorce?" CCF Council on Contemporary Families. Accessed April 29, 2024. https://sites.utexas.edu/contemporaryfamilies/2014/03/10/cohabitation-divorce-brief-report/

Lamm, M. "The Marriage Contract (Ketubah)." Accessed January 23, 2017. http://www.chabad.org/library/article_cdo/aid/465168/jewish/The-Marriage-Contract-Ketubah.htm.

Lamm. M. "The Marriage Ring." Accessed May 26, 2018. https://www.chabad.org/library/article_cdo/aid/481776/jewish/The-Marriage-Ring.htm.

Law.jrank. "Bilateral Contract." Accessed March 18, 2021. https://law.jrank.org/pages/4745/Bilateral-Contract.html.

Legal Dictionary. "Bilateral Contract." By Content Team. Accessed March 18, 2021. https://legaldictionary.net/bilateral-contract/.

MacPherson, R. C. "Whose fault was no-fault divorce?" Ruth Institute. Accessed August 31, 2019. http://www.ruthinstitute.org/ruth-speaks-out/whose-fault-was-no-fault-divorce.

Meacham (leBeit Yoreh), Tirzah. "Legal-Religious Status of the Married Woman." Shalvi/Hyman Encyclopedia of Jewish Women. 27 February 2009. Jewish Women's Archive. Accessed on July 4, 2024. https://jwa.org/encyclopedia/article/legal-religious-status-of-married-woman

Meek, R. "The Suzerain Vassal Treaty (Covenant) in the Old Testament." Russ Meek. 2024 Russell L. Meek. Site by Pilcrow. Reference Sandra Richter, *The Epic of Eden: A Christian Entry into the Old Testament* (Downers Grove, IL: IVP Academic, 2008). Accessed April 17, 2024. https://russmeek.com/2020/10/the-suzerain-vassal-treaty-covenant-in-the-old-testament/#_ftn5

Mikaloff, Justine. "Unilateral Contract." LegalMatch, LegalMatch Legal Writer. Accessed March 18, 2021. https://www.legalmatch.com/law-library/article/unilateral-contracts.html.

National Paralegal College. "Termination of the Power of Acceptance." (4) A qualified or conditional acceptance by the offeree. Accessed January 30, 2017. https://nationalparalegal.edu/public_documents/courseware_asp_files/contracts/MutualAssentOfferAndAcceptance/TerminationAcceptance.asp.

Page, R. "When is Divorce and Remarriage a Sin? #3. Divorce and Remarriage Today with Regards to Women: Introduction 3." Accessed January 12, 2017. https://www.logosapostolic.org/bible_study/RP2093-Divorce-women.htm#i3.

PBS. "THE ROMAN EMPIRE In the First Century." Women. Accessed April 23, 2024. https://www.pbs.org/empires/romans/empire/women.html

Piper, John. "God Created Man Male and Female. What Does It Mean to Be Complementarian?" Paragraph 2-3. Accessed April 2, 2018. https://www.desiringgod.org/messages/god-created-man-male-and-female-what-does-it-mean-to-be-complementarian.

Quimbee. "Acceptance by Performance." Accessed March 18, 2021. https://www.quimbee.com/keyterms/acceptance-by-performance.

Sanhe, Hu. "Chapter 3. Legal Concepts of the Insurance Contract." Revision f89211cd. Accessed March 18, 2021. https://life-and-health-insurance-license.readthedocs.io/Chapter3.%20Legal%20Concepts%20of%20the%20Insurance%20Contract/.

Schoch, D.A. "New Covenant Understanding. The Difference between Unilateral and Bilateral Covenants." Accessed December 11, 2017. https://newcovenantunderstanding.wordpress.com/2012/09/06/the-difference-between-unilateral-and-bilateral-covenants/.

Stanford University News Service. "Ancient Romans Led the Way in No-fault Divorce." Accessed March 17, 2015. http://news.stanford.edu/pr/91/911203Arc1041.html.

Soares, G., & Machado, S. "Opt-Out Clause in Not a Bank Check under Good Faith Lens." Scientific Research. Scientific Research Publishing Inc. Accessed April 29, 2024. https://www.scirp.org/journal/paperinformation?paperid=95332

The Conversation. "How 'Bride Price' Reinforces Negative Stereotypes: a Ghanaian Case Study." Accessed March 18, 2021. https://theconversation.com/how-bride-price-reinforces-negative-stereotypes-a-ghanaian-case-study-120337.

Thismatter.com. "Insurance Contracts: Consideration, Unilateral Contracts (conditional contracts)." William C. Spaulding. Accessed September 25, 2017. http://thismatter.com/money/insurance/insurance-contracts.htm.

Threedy, D., Kogan, T. & Dewald, A. "9. Contracts: Consideration." © University of Utah S. J. Quinney College. Center for Innovation in Legal Education. Accessed February 2, 2018. https://www.youtube.com/watch?v=Id-PabUby5Ck&t=2s.

Trovato, Nina. "The Truth About Father Bias in Family Courts." Everyday Feminism. Accessed January 30, 2019. https://everydayfeminism.com/2013/08/bias-against-fathers/.

Walson, James. "When are Unilateral Termination Rights in a Commercial Lease Enforceable?" JDSUPRA. Copyright 2020 JD Supra, LLC. Accessed March 17, 2020. https://www.jdsupra.com/legalnews/when-are-unilateral-termination-rights-90076/.

Weiss, Susan. "Divorce: The Halakhic Perspective. Jewish Woman: A Comprehensive Historical Encyclopedia." Jewish Woman's Archive. Articles: "Biblical Origins and the Unilateral, No-Fault Grounds for Divorce. Dispensation to Take a Second Wife." Accessed October 30, 2017. https://jwa.org/encyclopedia/article/divorce-halakhic-perspective.